TACKLING
MANAGEMENT

SELF CO... RS

JUSTINE BALLARD AND ELIZABETH FERGUSON

The Campaign for Learning is an independent charity, working to put learning at the heart of social inclusion. As part of its work, the Campaign supports organisations to build a culture of learning. It runs National Learning at Work Day, the largest annual celebration of workplace learning and skills. It also co-ordinates the National Workplace Learning Network, which supports members to engage employees in learning. The network shares information, runs events and offers downloadable resources.
For more information visit: www.campaignforlearning.org.uk

Acknowledgements

Thanks to Denis Betts, Skills Coach at Gloucestershire Rugby Club for his input, passion for coaching and helpful insights into the world of sports coaching.

Thanks also to:
Giles Mountford
The staff at Campaign for Learning
Dr Michael Carroll
Dr Ilona Boniwell
Dr Beverley Hawkins
John East
Pauline Laybourne

First published 2009

Campaign for Learning   and   Southgate Publishers Ltd
19, Buckingham Street   The Square, Sandford
London   Crediton, Devon
WC2N 6EF   EX17 4LW
www.campaignforlearning.org.uk   www.southgatepublishers.co.uk

Printed and bound in Great Britain by Stephens & George Print Group, Merthyr Tydfil, Wales

British Library Cataloguing in Publication Data
A CIP catalogue record for this book is available from the British Library

ISBN 9 781903 107 19 5

Contents

Introduction

This booklet has been written to help you as a line manager, to manage yourself, your development and your own resilience.

Merging the experience of corporate coaches Justine Ballard and Elizabeth Ferguson and with insights from Denis Betts, a rugby skills coach, you'll learn practical ways to build resilience, continually improve and to 'last the management course'.

Because you are more than just the tasks and objectives that you carry out, we take the sports coach approach of working with you on both a physical and mental level. With resources and a 'to do' list, you'll also have the opportunity to reflect on where you are now and where you can go in the future.

As a manager you are the key link between the business's objectives and its resources. This wonderful role offers you the opportunity to drive the business forward, be more involved in developing the organisation's aims, as well as being key to empowering your own staff and communicating a shared goal.

Whilst this is exciting, you'll face many types of challenges and not all of them will be around how to run a meeting, write an appraisal or delegate to staff. There may be times when the pressure is on, your energy is limited and your own learning and performance reaches a plateau.

In the sports world, athletes and players have coaches who spend a lot of time monitoring their performance, measuring their fitness and feeding back on areas that will make huge improvements to their performance.

In the business world, this role falls (to an extent) to your manager and you may be one of many people that they manage. Occasionally you may have access to a coach at work, who will give you the space to reflect and help you focus on the goals that you bring to them.

In both cases, coaching relies heavily on building rapport, trust and commitment and using questioning and reflection to gain self-awareness. During this book we give you time to reflect and increase your self-awareness through asking you questions at the end of each section. You'll effectively be empowering yourself through self coaching.

The coaching approach

We want you to feel empowered and to feel able to take responsibility for your own performance. As a manager you will be faced with a wide variety of situations you may not have met before. You may have had some training or advice about *what to do*, but you have probably had little or no guidance on how you will feel or react in these situations on a personal level – *how you will be*. In many ways that is the difference between training and coaching.

Training teaches you how to do something, coaching helps you to be at your best to do it.

Self coaching gives you the ability to empower yourself to:

- Honestly explore what's going on for you
- Identify the options you have
- Agree with yourself about what you want to change
- Decide what actions to take
- Gather any resources or support you might need
- Make changes so that you last the course.

Coaching offers you a personal space which allows you to look at your talents and attributes without embarrassment or shyness and gives you the self-motivation to want to make more of them as you grow as a manager. The process can also help you identify those areas that are not your natural strengths (we all have them) and decide how you can compensate for them by using your strengths, or, if they are absolutely essential skills or attributes, how you might develop them.

However, this is not all quite as easy as it may first appear! In the coaching world we talk about 'coachability' as being essential for coaching to be effective and this is true whether you are working directly with a coach or if you are self coaching.

There are three elements to 'coachability':

Ready: you need to know what you want to achieve; what your goal is for your coaching. As an example, it might be 'being more effective with your staff'.

Willing: you need to be willing to make the changes or take the actions required to reach your goal. So, in this example, it may be that to be more effective with your staff you will have to get detailed feedback from them, and then make changes to your attitudes and behaviours based on their feedback.

Able: you need to have the ability and resources to make the changes. For most people this one is easy as it is down to you as an individual.

Earlier we mentioned responsibility, and this is a key area where coaching differs from training. In training, the trainer has a responsibility for imparting skills in the best way they can to enable the trainees to learn. In coaching, the responsibility for thinking about the issues, identifying options and taking the actions lies completely with you. There isn't anyone else involved and that is why the 'ready, willing and able' is so important. If you are not fully committed to making changes to achieve your goal then the coaching will not be effective.

However, when you are committed and you do self coach to make those changes, your sense of personal achievement and self-confidence knows no bounds.

As you work through this book it's useful to bear in mind that you will find some questions more thought-provoking than others and some questions much harder to answer. Often the hardest questions to answer are the ones that allow the most significant changes to occur, so it is worth spending time thinking about the hard questions if you want to make big changes with sustainable results.

Some questions will seem easy and obvious, but before you move on from them, spend a moment or two asking yourself if your answers are really honest, or whether there is more to explore? Also, ask yourself what assumptions you are making with your easy answer. Is there another way of looking at this?

Great coaching leaves no stone unturned, so do not be discouraged if you sometimes find it difficult or tiring; these are sure signs that you are committed to your coaching and that changes are going to be made. Often coaching focuses on making changes to behaviours that you have been perfecting all of your life, so it is hardly surprising it takes some effort to break these habits. If you do find things getting tough, here are a few top tips to make the going easier:

- Break your goal down into smaller chunks you can make progress with.
- Enlist the support and encouragement of friends and family to spur you on by telling them what you have achieved so far.
- Go and have some fun or do something totally different that allows your mind to switch off.

? Questions to get you started ?

This section helps you to develop your self coaching goals and know where you need to target your energies first. Just answer the warm-up questions below and identify your current behaviours. Be really honest, and notice where you need to focus your efforts as you go through the book.

Each question relates to a particular section of the book that splits into three main sections:

* Building resilience
* Constantly improving
* Lasting the course.

Questions	Always	Sometimes	Never
Resilience: When you have setbacks, how often do you quickly bounce back?			
Resilience: Do you have people that you can talk to or get advice from when you need to?			
Resilience: Are you able to recognise how other people are feeling and respond appropriately?			
Resilience: How often do you feel anxious?			
Improving: Can you listen to someone's opinion without being defensive?			
Improving: Do you enjoy getting feedback from people?			
Improving: Do you enjoy trying new and different ways of doing things?			
Improving: Do you list and acknowledge what you achieve over the year?			
Improving: On a daily basis, how often do you learn something new?			
Lasting: Are you aware of, and conscious of, your core skills and abilities?			
Lasting: How often do you feel confident about your ability to perform your job?			
Lasting: How often do you stretch yourself with jobs or deadlines when you don't need to?			
Lasting: Do you take ten minutes at the start of each day to prepare for what's ahead?			
Lasting: How committed are you to taking action to reach your goals?			

Recognise the questions that were harder to answer and look to specifically take some actions when you get to that part in the book. Be honest with yourself about whether you're willing to take action and make changes. Think of one small action that you can do today that will have an impact on tomorrow.

And one last thing before we go on... every professional coach knows it is essential to have lots of fun when you are coaching. So be open to laugh at yourself sometimes, to smile at what you could work towards and to celebrate what you achieve. Coaching is the most inspiring, exciting journey – enjoy it!

Building Resilience

Being able to recover and recuperate quickly from changes, challenges, illness or unforeseen events is a very useful ability. When these things happen it is important to learn from them and let the emotion go. It's useful to remember that you cannot always control the environmental factors, only your reaction to them.

You can build your resilience through:

- Building your emotional intelligence
- Building a strong network
- Managing your own anxiety and reactions
- Ensuring your own wellbeing.

Develop your emotional intelligence

Emotional intelligence (EQ) reflects your ability to understand and manage your own emotions as well as being able to recognise and empathise with others. Even if you have an incredibly high IQ you'll also need EQ to be able to manage people and deal with everyday social situations competently.

'A setback or
failure is nothing
more than an
unexpected
outcome. Learn
to have fun
and enjoy the
unexpected.'
Elizabeth Ferguson

**Building
resilience!**

In his book, *Working With Emotional Intelligence*, Daniel Goleman argues that workplace competencies based on emotional intelligence play a strong role in star performance, whilst leading coach Sir John Whitmore sees EQ as becoming an increasingly important leadership skill as organisations change and become less hierarchical.

To understand your own EQ, consider how you manage your emotions and the strategies that you use when needing solace and balance. EQ is about:

- Recognising how you feel and what has triggered that.
- Realising how you motivate yourself and what your drivers are.
- Recognising and understanding emotions in others. Can you step into their shoes for a moment?
- Assessing the way you manage relationships and manage emotions in others.

Take the sportsman who has just lost the most important game in the season. Despite his huge disappointment, he has to respond appropriately to the people who have paid to see him, he has to communicate and empathise with the team and his manager, and most of all he has to deal with the emotions and move on so that he can go out and play in the next game truly believing that he can and will win.

As a manager and leader you will need to manage your own emotions whilst also empathising, motivating and empowering your staff. Strong and successful leaders have been shown to possess these skills. They are able to clearly communicate, empathise with those around and respond to situations appropriately.

On reflection...

- Did anything happen today that triggered negative emotions?
- How did you deal with those emotions...? Did you speak to people? Withdraw? Take action? React with anger? Reassess the situation and move on?
- Think of a time when you have been really motivated. What environmental and internal factors contributed to this?
- How easily are you able to empathise with others in your team?

Build a supportive network

If you look out for them, you'll likely meet a wide range of interesting, experienced and knowledgeable people through work, at events and through friends and family.

Mutually supportive relationships with a range of very different people can be helpful when you have bad days, or times when you don't know how to deal with things. They will be there to talk to, laugh with, get advice from and generally seek reassurance from.

Build up your network through:

- Talking to and spending time with, colleagues outside of work.
- Finding a mentor – this might be someone who is in the same business area as you who has more experience and knowledge.
- Being open to having coffee with consultants and freelancers you have worked with even when you don't currently have work for them. They can often become friends as well as colleagues and will have an outside perspective on things.
- When you meet people, building rapport through asking them questions about themselves; share common experiences.
- Identifying people who are good at what you do and research how they are resilient.
- Attending a relevant seminar or professional event and talk to the people beside you.
- Joining a network of people in a similar field or role, such as the Campaign for Learning's National Workplace Learning Network.
- Offering to be a mentor for others.
- Using a coach!

It's important to make sure that your network consists of people who are positive and supportive and are able to see potential in situations. Negative people will drain your energy and won't be able to give you unbiased and constructive feedback.

Consider having members of your network who are more experienced or very different from you in their outlook so that their point of view can stretch your own thinking and perspective.

A strong network will help you feel stronger and supported, part of a team and therefore able to take risks and try new ways of working.

On reflection...

- Is your present network of friends generally positive and supportive?
- Who can you talk to when you need a sounding board?
- Is there someone whose work and attitude you admire who you could ask to be your mentor?
- How can you extend your network with people who will stretch your thinking?

Manage your anxiety

Stop and manage your own anxiety when you feel overloaded, confused and challenged.

Sometimes being a manager means that you have to take on more responsibilities at short notice and manage a wide range of issues from HR to finance. If you're rushing between meetings, dealing with tricky people issues and running out of hours, you may feel anxious and tired. It's important to realise when your state has changed and recognise the impact this has on how you react to people and challenges.

The good news is that there are things you can do to help yourself in this situation.

Breathe: Your physiology can have a huge impact on your thoughts and your ability to deal with stress. Often we don't think about our breathing, and it can be short and shallow. Breathing deeply is calming and helps the body deal with the symptoms of stress.

Act 'as if': Holding your body 'as if' you are feeling confident and in control will not only convince those around you that you can handle it, but also yourself. It's hard for your body to be anxious when it's acting confidently. For instance act 'as if' in these ways:

- Think of how you are when you are confident.
- Stand and hold yourself as you do when you feel confident and comfortable.
- Slow down your breathing.
- Replicate the tone and volume of your confident voice.
- Make eye contact with others in the same way that you do when you feel assured and confident.

Remember who you are when you're at your best and then replicate it!

'I am': Affirmations are a way of reminding yourself of your strengths, of the type of person you want to be and a way of giving yourself a pep talk. It follows on from acting 'as if'. Remember, your focus and thoughts will drive your actions, so if you tell yourself I AM confident and capable again and again, you start to believe it and you will act and feel confident and capable.

When you feel anxious or stressed try one of the following:

- Breathe deeply (filling your stomach and breathing out through your mouth slowly).
- Stand up straight and look up.
- Develop positive affirmations for yourself – e.g. I am a strong, positive, capable person.
- Remind yourself that whatever happens, you'll handle it. Your attitude is the key to your success.
- Find a quiet space or go outside – walk around the block.
- Close your eyes for a moment and then spot six different colours around the room.

On reflection...

- How do you act when you are anxious? What would others notice about you?
- What action can you take in future to manage your anxiety?
- How is your physiology right now? Notice how you are feeling and holding yourself. Now do something completely different and notice how that feels.
- Practise breathing in through the nose, feeling your stomach expand. Then breathe out slowly through your mouth. Repeat that 10 times and notice how you feel.

Manage your well-being

You can manage your own well-being through deliberately searching out things that you enjoy, that make you laugh and people that raise your spirits.

The Oxford Dictionary describes 'well-being' as the state of being comfortable, healthy, or happy. By understanding what energises us, we can more actively affect our own happiness and well-being levels and avoid situations that sap our energy.

Dr Ilona Boniwell of the East London University has concluded from her research that there are four key roads to enhancing your well-being:

1. Positive emotions	Increasing our joy, contentment, love and interest
2. Relationships	Married people tend to be happier! Focus on those you love
3. Engagement	Finding things that immerse you, being in the moment
4. Meaning	Focusing beyond oneself and making a difference to others

Many people have asked the question, "Can we learn our way to happiness?" The answer is - absolutely! We may not be able to change our circumstances or events that take place, and the environment that we are in will always have an impact, but we do have choices and we can take action to help ourselves.

Research shows that to give yourself a better chance of being happy you need to:

- Play and be creative
- Share and explore with others
- Find out new information; explore the world; expand the self
- Exercise – the endorphins are a powerful anti-depressant
- Stretch yourself realistically - avoid the rut of boredom
- Do things that contribute to the bigger world picture or to other people's well-being
- Take action to move towards your goals and vision
- Learn from setbacks and recognise your strengths
- Give the gift of time to people you care about and to yourself
- Enjoy strong relationships
- Get regular medical check-ups
- Restrict your 'on-screen' time.

Researchers suggest that if happiness scales are to be believed, you might also want to avoid middle age and raising teenagers!

On reflection...

- What brings you joy and makes you smile?
- What really engages you? (What are you good at?)
- What is meaningful to you? (What provides you with purpose?)
- What can you do now to get more of these regularly into your life?

Most of us are just about as happy as we make up our minds to be.
William Adams

Constantly improving

The reality is that we live in a world where change is constant. Technology advances continually and organisations have a much faster turnover of staff, projects and management. By learning and growing from daily situations and taking up opportunities to learn and develop, you'll be better placed for challenges, changes and promotion.

If you start from the premise that you will never know everything, and will never be 'perfect', your life can become a quest to learn as much as possible.

Ways to improve:

- Learn to learn
- Be open to feedback
- Be curious and try new things
- Acknowledge the wins.

If you answered 'never' or 'sometimes' to the 'Constantly Improving' questions (see page 7), this section will help you focus on those areas and suggest ideas to help you develop.

"We learn by example and by direct experience because there are real limits to the adequacy of verbal instruction. "
Malcolm Gladwell, Blink: The Power of Thinking Without Thinking, 2005

> *As a 'recovered' perfectionist I've learnt that being imperfect is just fine and that I don't need to know everything to move on and up to new levels.*
> **Elizabeth Ferguson**

Learning to learn

The Campaign for Learning sees *'learning how to learn'* as being every bit as important as learning itself. We don't always know today what we may need to learn tomorrow. However, if we understand how we learn best, what motivates us to learn, and how to set learning goals we will meet any challenge.

To help the 'learning to learn' process, The Campaign for Learning has developed the 5 Rs framework, which links closely with the coaching process. The 5 Rs describe key skills, attributes and dispositions that we need to be effective learners. They are:

Readiness: knowing your motivation, setting your goals, understanding your learning environment.

Resourcefulness: using the information, assessing your preferences, communicating, and trying different approaches.

Resilience: being emotionally aware, proceeding when stuck, asking questions.

Responsibility: ownership of your own development, learning with others, making the best use of learning opportunities, being a learning role model.

Reflectiveness: asking questions, observing, spotting patterns, and evaluating learning.

Learning can take place absolutely everywhere; at work, at home or with friends, on the bus, train or sitting in the park or with your children. Remember to look for, and acknowledge, the opportunities to learn; it's more than training, classrooms and on-line courses; it comes through new experiences, talking to people and sometimes just doing day-to-day tasks.

Enjoy learning through:

- Reading books and professional magazines
- Attending seminars
- Talking to people
- Asking questions
- Doing something new
- Digging deeper when you see something relevant mentioned
- Visiting websites
- Free E-Learning (such as BBC Learning)
- Joining professional organisations
- Finding a mentor
- Coaching
- Watching people (preferably without staring!).

The moment you think you know it all is the moment you regress and stagnate. Constant curiosity will widen your world, your opportunities and your toolbox. It also keeps you young!

On reflection...

* What was the most curious thing you encountered today that you want to understand or learn more about?
* What positive action did you take today to learn something?
* Are you a member of any relevant professional bodies?
* What would you like to learn about tomorrow?

Being open to feedback

One of the best ways to improve is to listen to feedback whenever it's offered – and if it isn't, ask for it.

Listen to what people say with an open mind. Feedback is available through your boss, your colleagues, your family, your friends; in fact anyone you interact with. Ask them questions about their views without being defensive. All feedback is good feedback.

The other form of feedback is experience. You often grow and learn more when things go wrong than when they go right. Learn from those events and use that experience; don't be embarrassed by it.

An example of feedback on a wider scale comes from the sports team. Each week its performance is scrutinised and appraised – by their fans, their family, their friends, the press, their coaches and the board members. The fans' support is everything; the coach will have specific and constructive criticism; the press might revel in the team's performance one week but then mercilessly criticise it the next. The players need to be able to listen and then discern what can help them improve and what they need to ignore.

You will also need to judge what feedback is most useful and helpful. Everyone will have a different opinion, but you will have a strong sense of who you are and what your strengths are. Therefore listen, learn, note useful action points and weigh up the evidence - both the good and the bad!

When giving feedback to others, remember to give it context, explain why you are giving it and make sure you have rapport with the person you're giving it to. Tell them what was great.... specific ways that it could be improved and an overall summation.

Feedback is a person's perception of your actions and not the reality. However, by asking more in-depth questions of people, and giving their comments thought and consideration, you can become more aware of your strengths and weaknesses and whether your efforts and actions are seen in the way you want them to be.

> *Feedback is the breakfast of champions.*
> **Ken Blanchard**

Remember that there is a difference between feedback and verbal abuse. Feedback is constructive and specific whereas verbal abuse is general and personal. When receiving feedback you should get a sense of what and how you can do better rather than just what was wrong.

On reflection...

* What was the last piece of feedback you received; how did you react to that?
* How might you ask for feedback more often?
* How often do you give constructive and helpful feedback to your colleagues?

Try new ways

If something is not working – try doing it differently, experiment and learn.

Experimenting and trying new things can open up a whole new world. You'll probably find a more effective way of working; you might meet new people or learn about a different aspect of your work. You'll definitely increase your opportunities to develop and grow as well as stretch your 'innovation' muscle. When looking to change something you might want to:

* Do your research – list all of the possibilities that exist and then find what is appropriate for you. There is usually more than one route to achieving your goal – just because it's been done that way before does not mean that it's the best way.
* Think about who has done it well before, what they did and how they did it. Is there anything that you can learn from them?
* Read up on your subject – what information do you need to increase your options?
* Ask for feedback from those around you. What would they like to see done differently?
* Be brave.

Situations move on due to both people and technology. This means that solutions need to move onwards also. Being a leader and pioneer can be challenging but can also provide you with excitement, learning and the chance to show your leadership skills.

On reflection...

- What isn't working for you right now? .... Specifically?
- What exactly is the outcome you are seeking? Is there another way to get there?
- How many different approaches have you investigated and tried?
- What are you doing purely because it was done that way before? Is there any way in which you can improve that?

When the first sports coaches brought in ballet training to improve players' dexterity and balance, or hypnosis to help with focus and goal-setting, they were seen as slightly mad – but now both techniques are used to great effect on a regular basis...

" Winners compare their achievements with their goals, while losers compare their achievements with those of other people. "
Nido Qubein, President of High Point University

Acknowledge and celebrate the wins!

Recognise the small steps and celebrate the large achievements.
It's important to have big goals to aim for, but also to acknowledge how close you are to achieving them. Be aspirational whilst enjoying and acknowledging the journey.
For instance, you may aspire to be an entertaining and motivational speaker, but give yourself a pat on the back when you give your first presentation to more than ten people… or completely on your own.

Habits to develop

- Have a list of actions and tick them off when completed – it reinforces the feeling of progression and achievement.
- Remember to recognise the achievements and progression of your staff. They need to be acknowledged for moving towards their goals and thus motivated to continue.
- Have a clear idea of what the achievement looks like and feels like…. How will you know when you've achieved it – what's the moment?
- Enjoy the moment of achievement; you've worked hard to achieve it, so mentally revel in it. Note how it feels, your energy levels, what happens.

When you are working towards a large goal it can sometimes feel overwhelming and unobtainable. Each small win takes you closer to that larger goal. Enjoy it.

On reflection...

- What have you achieved today?
- How do you acknowledge your achievements?
- How do you acknowledge others' achievements?

The beauty is in the moment – you've worked hard to achieve it so acknowledge how it feels. It's the start of you becoming even better again.
Denis Betts

> Real people – real reflections: "Last week I found a list of everything I'd achieved between 2003 and 2006. I'd really forgotten how far I'd advanced, and was also spurred on by the fact that I'd achieved some of the goals that I'd put down. This has inspired me to start a new list."
> **Janine**

Lasting the course

At work as on the pitch, it's important to manage your energy, to be able to 'up your game' when needed and ensure you don't feel overburdened or suffer from stress. A successful manager is proactive, creative and responsive, and for this you need to be strong and motivated.

There are a number of ways to do this:

- You prepare by warming up
- Play to your strengths
- Relax – you know what you're doing
- You practise what you need to be good at.

Daily warm-up

It's important to prepare yourself for each day, taking a moment to understand your goals and plan your time as much as possible. We all know that athletes never rush straight into a full-on sprint or compete without warming up. They prepare their muscles so that they are more agile. The increased blood flow helps them to become more mentally focussed and in the right frame of mind.

Sports men and women will mentally prepare through visualising success. Because they've already practised and built up the muscles and knowledge before hand they will practise mentally and repeat the success again and again in their mind. For instance basketball players see mental rehearsal as an important way to practise getting hoops. This is because experiencing success increases confidence, even if that experience is imagined. By having a clear picture of what you want to achieve it is much easier for you to achieve it.

Take a moment at the start of each day to prepare for whatever is coming up. By choosing your attitude for the day you can choose how successful the day will be. For example, are you positive, ready to make things happen, happy?

Also consider your environment. How organised is your desk and diary? Take some time out before you start to look through your diary, print off the day's appointments, organise your desk so that the papers you need are clear and ready to hand and write down tasks as they come up in your day book. Write down your tasks for the day in your day book – and key conversations you have and the actions coming from them. You can also paste your daily diary in it if you use Outlook. It helps if you keep a record of when you have completed things, as well as any ideas and thoughts that crop up during the day.

Breathe and relax. Stress has many effects and will undoubtedly have an impact on how you do your work. Begin the day with some slow breathing to help energise yourself, relax your shoulders and consider visualising how you want things to happen that day. Imagine yourself achieving key actions and mentally walk through the major activities and events. Visualisation can be used for: job interviews, presentations, athletic performances, sales calls and teaching.

See it; believe it; achieve it!

> *Real people – real reflections:*
> I was introduced to the daybook when I worked in advertising sales and I've used one ever since. By having a tick list of tasks for the day or week, and keeping notes of important phone calls, it's easier to acknowledge my achievements, to be clear about dates and to have a reference when needed.
> **Justine**

Tip: Visualisation should always focus on what you want. Be specific, vivid and involve movement. Include the moment where you know you've achieved it.

On reflection...

- What attitude will you decide to start your day with tomorrow?
- Did you take time to mentally warm up and think through your objectives for the day?
- What can you do today to make your work area/desk more comfortable for tomorrow?
- Notice your breathing. Is it deep and even or shallow and fast?

Play to strengths

Play to your strengths when you're playing and working at full rate.

Through the experience of having worked your way through the business or organisation, you'll have discovered that there are certain traits that people admire and respect in you and parts of the job that you find easier and more satisfying.

Take a moment to understand and write down the characteristics and attitudes that make you the manager and leader you are, for instance:

- Are you great with people?
- Do you have fantastic organisational skills?
- Do you love detail?
- Are you action orientated or more strategic?
- Are you collaborative and team orientated?
- Can you develop the talents of others?
- What are your core values?
- What is it that you are interested in and passionate about?

These things are all part of your core and will drive your energies and effectiveness. Skills and knowledge can be learnt or improved and built around the core 'you'.

In some sports a player is hired for a particular key skill such as speed or strength.

Think about how you contribute to the overall goal. How do you share your strengths and how do you teach others?
Denis Betts

Each player is there to contribute a different aspect of the game but ultimately they will also need to play as part of a wider team.

You'll need to remember though that you'll never be all things to all people. Be aware of what you need to do to be at least competent in all aspects but also remember you were hired for certain abilities, strengths and your personality, so promote and build on them.

By realising the part you play within the organisation and how your strengths contribute, you can work better with others to meet the overall objectives. Remember also to look to recognise and acknowledge the people that work for you and structure your team to play to those strengths.

On reflection...

- What drives you? What part of the job do you really enjoy?
- What is your greatest strength?
- Do other people believe that that is your strength?
- What action can you take to become an expert in that area?
- How can you share your knowledge and skills with others?

Relax – you know your job!

It's easy to get caught up in the sidelines and to waste your energy on the things that really aren't that important. Running around might make you visible but not productive. Make sure that you're in the right place at the right time otherwise you have to waste energy getting there. Know which direction you're travelling in – what are the overall goals and what do they look like? Focus on what has positive impact and if questioned, explain that you have prioritised.

Real people – real reflections:
What drives me is making people happy. I really enjoy meeting and building strong relationships with colleagues and stakeholders and providing good customer service.
Pauline

This is incredibly important when you're working and playing at full pace; you can feel your energy becoming drained; and you are becoming stressed or pulled in many directions.

Stop – breathe and ask yourself – what am I here to do? What do I need to achieve right now? How can I best affect what I'm doing? Anything that isn't going to specifically help you reach that action should be delegated, delayed or deferred.

In sports the 4Cs of concentration, confidence, control and commitment are considered the key mental attributes for success. These are also so clearly important in the workplace.

Concentration   ability to maintain focus and not get side tracked

Confidence   belief in one's abilities and skills

Control   being able to control your emotions regardless of distraction

Commitment   ability to continue working to agreed goals.

On reflection...

- What activity took up most of your time today?
- Did that activity directly contribute to your objectives and goals?
- Which of the four Cs should you focus on and improve?
- Did you have time to reflect and plan today or was it just action?

Real people – real reflections:

I spent most of today replying to emails, fire fighting and helping someone else with their objectives. So I've just blocked out some time in my diary for tomorrow to plan for our away day which has been on my 'to do' list for a week.
Celia

Build up your stamina through practice

Athletes and sports people train for the big race and all-important game – they see this as their opportunity to shine and step up to the challenge. What is your race or game? When are you most pressurised? Instead of seeing challenging situations as stressful, see them as your chance to succeed and use all the muscles (skills and knowledge) that you've built up.

Just as athletes do, you can increase your 'muscles' and prepare for the big game. During the less frantic times – when you're not working at peak performance, practise key skills that will help you when it comes to busier times. For instance:

Tip: When something seems really hard going stop and ask yourself, 'What's the easiest way of doing this?' You'll be amazed at what you come up with.

- Stretch your brain through tighter deadlines than needed
- Practise speed-reading
- Consciously use and practise your rapport-building skills
- Download useful management information from websites such as the Chartered Management Institute
- Collate facts or information on your business area that might be useful
- Practise skills not often used like presenting
- Be consciously aware of how people's body language reflects their thoughts and moods
- Practise producing charts from data.

Our skills are like muscles; they need to be used on a regular basis. It is experience and practice that enables you to do things more efficiently and quickly and if practised enough, these skills can become second nature. Remember, small changes can have a big impact.

On reflection...

* What muscle/skill if any, did you build on today?
* What did you learn from that?
* What skills or knowledge can you build up in future?

Commit to your goals

Being clear about what you want to achieve is an important element of moving forward. Visualising what that achievement would look like and the point of success is also key. The starting point is understanding why you want to go for the goal. If it is something you think you *should* do, rather than what you really want to do, then you probably won't be sufficiently committed to achieve it. So unless you are ready to take action and do something that moves you towards that goal, reassess how committed you are to it and whether it is the right goal for you now.

Whilst this is all common sense, it's all too easy to get caught up in our day-to-day lives where we are working, parenting and helping others and so forget to make time for ourselves. Promises to other people will often take precedence over promises to ourselves; how many times have you made the effort to meet up with someone you have given a commitment to, but have found a reason why getting to the gym, going for a walk, reading a book is simply impossible to fit in for yourself. Your well-being is just as important as others', so start honouring those commitments you make to yourself.

It's also worth considering whether you own your decisions and actions or see yourself at the mercy of others. If we acknowledge that everything that happens always has a cause, a reason for happening, then by putting ourselves at the 'cause' (assuming that we make things happen and not other people or other things), we give ourselves more options and more power to progress. It's easy to find reasons why things don't happen, but the truth is, almost all of the time we can choose what we make happen if we dare.

If you have a goal that you just don't seem to be progressing towards:

- Think of one thing (no matter how small) that you can do today that will get you closer to your goal.
- Remind yourself about the gain or benefit you will be getting from achieving the goal.
- Remember that you can make things happen – don't wait for others.
- If time is an issue – just find ten minutes a day to devote to moving things forward.
- This is a promise to yourself – take it as seriously as the promises you make to others.

On reflection...

- Take a moment and assess if that really is the right goal for you – how do you feel when you think about it?
- Are you waiting for other things to be in place before you start? If so, what can you do in the meantime?
- Can you create a plan with small steps which will take you towards your goal?
- How much time in a week do you devote to your own growth and progress?
- What else can you do to take control and make this happen for you?

Summary

As a manager you are much more than the tasks that you do. You are a role model, a leader and the link between the needs of the organisation and the needs of people. To do this successfully you'll need resilience, stamina and the drive to keep getting better.

By self coaching and taking responsibility for your own well-being and development you'll send out the message to other people that your well-being and development are important. You'll be able to respond more quickly and in a way that you choose and be the best that you can be. You also model the importance of self-development and self-awareness to your staff.

To help you reflect, review and set goals, surround yourself with positive and constructive friends and colleagues. Stop and ask yourself key questions when you are unsure. Focus on how you want to be and then act 'as if'!

As with any learning, the best way to remember all that you've read here and embed productive new behaviours is to take action as soon as possible.

As we said earlier, its amazing how one small change or new behaviour today can impact on tomorrow. The questions at the beginning and throughout the book will give you an indication of where you can make the biggest differences. Pick one or two things either from the 'things you can do' list below, or actions that have come up for you whilst reading this book and try them out; see how they fit and be aware of any changes.

To help you delve deeper, we've also included some of the useful and interesting websites that we've come across as well as some of the books that have had an impact on us in some way and at some point in our careers.

Enjoy, and good luck on your journey.

Things you can do:

- Act as if you are the manager that you want to be
- Ask for feedback and listen with an open mind
- See every day as a learning opportunity
- Make a list of your core attributes and skills
- Practise deep and slow breathing
- Find a mentor
- Use a coach
- Use a day book
- Speed reading: read a book or go on a course
- Write down everything you've achieved, the courses you've attended and the dreams that you've realised over the last three years. Acknowledge your success
- Prepare by playing important events through in your mind as you wish them to happen
- Take time to arrange your work area so that it works for you
- Stretch your muscles....all of them
- Keep a special book to use for writing down useful facts, figures and websites
- Join a professional organisation
- Acknowledge your staff's achievements and thank them
- Assess your nutrition – make it work for you
- Be aware of your body language – stand tall
- Ask questions – don't assume
- Make clear, defined, SMART goals that you can see and believe in
- Share and swap knowledge with your colleagues
- Attend a leadership course or read about different leadership styles
- Reflect at the end of each major piece of work or meeting on what went well and what went not so well. How would you do it differently in future?
- Remember that the biggest choice you can make is how you react to an event
- Play games – be creative, paint, draw, make models – it has to be enjoyable not saleable!
- Laugh – see the funny side.

Energy questionnaire

What should you do more of and what should you try and avoid?

	Physically	Emotionally	Mentally	Spiritually
What energises me?				
What saps my energy?				
What would help energise me?				
What do I need to change in my life?				
	Physical energy Eating, Drinking Sleeping Physical Fitness Breaks Ourselves	**Emotional Energy** Self confidence Relationships Empathy Dealing with stress Negative emotions	**Mental energy** Time management Creativity Thinking Skills Challenging the brain Mental preparation	**Spiritual energy** Commitment Enthusiasm Values Building character A purpose beyond

Courtesy of Dr Michael Carroll, based upon Loeh and Swartz's four types of energy in 'The Power of Full Engagement'.

Resources

Books we've enjoyed

Success Comes in Cans
Kriss Akabusi & Tricia Hartley
Continuum Press 2006

The Definitive Book of Body Language: how to read others' attitudes by their gestures
Allan Pease and Barbara Pease
Orion, New edition 2005

The New Leaders – Transforming the art of leadership / Emotional Intelligence
Daniel Goleman, Richard Bayatzis, Anne McKee
Timer Warner paperbacks 2003

Presenting Magically
David Shephard & Tad James
Crown House Publicity 2001

Play to your Strengths
Donald O'Clifton & Paula Nelson
Piatkus Books 1994

Positive Psychology in a Nutshell
Dr Ilona Boniwell
PWBC 2nd edition 2008

Influencing with Integrity
Genie Laborde
Crown House Publishing

The Food Doctor
Ian Marber
Dorling Kindersley 2008

Mind Games, Inspirational Lessons from the World's Biggest Sport Stars
Sir Clive Woodward, Jeff Grout & Sarah Perrin Capstone 2006

First Break all the Rules
Now Discover Your Strengths Marcus Buckingham & Curt Coffman
Pocket Books 2005

The Resilience Factor
Reivich, K. & Shatte, A.
Broadway Books Reprint 2003

The Art of Possibility
Rosamund Zander & Ben Zander
Harvard Business School Press 2000

Happier
Tal Ben-Shahar
McGraw-Hill Professional 2007

NLP at Work
Sue Knight
Nicholas Brealey Publishing Ltd
Revised 2002

Feel the Fear and Do It Anyway.
Susan Jeffers
Vermillion 20th Anniversary 2007

Breathwork
Swami Ambikananda Saraswati
Thorsons 2001

The Inner Game of Work
The Inner Game of Tennis
Timothy Gallway
Mass Market Paperbook 1982

The Power of Verbal Intelligence
The Power of Creative Intelligence
The Power of Social Intelligence
Tony Buzan
Thorsons 2002